teen LIFE GOALS guide

by LYNN MERRIN

teen CONFIDENCE guide

by LYNN MERRIN

Introduction

Confidence is an inspiring book designed to
assist you to make positive change in your life.

Take a personal journey of consideration,
beyond the physical,
to further understand the subconscious
mind from a metaphysical viewpoint.

Confidence is the first of four motivational guides,
complete with inspiring verses,
daily affirmations and creative visualisations.
These verses are charged with Reiki energy to enhance
these personally empowering processes.

Looking at the various aspects of expression of Confidence consider the following:

confidence	comes with belief in our ability to succeed
self acceptance	comes with love and faith in ourselves
individuality	being who we really are
independence	making it on our own
poise	inner calm mentally/emotionally/physical
calm	control over our emotions and mind
inner peace	comes with faith that all is as it should be
trust	in ourselves as the creator of our destiny
faith	that we have made the right decisions
grace	is calm self assured dignity
posture	the position in which a person holds their body
dress	clothes of a particular type worn in a particular way
smile	to appear to be in state of happiness or enjoying pleasure
charm	the power to delight or attract people
handshake	a gesture of gripping or shaking a hand as a greeting
eye contact	the act of looking directly into the eyes of other person
voice	the sound produced in speech and song

Confidence

Confidence is a belief or self assurance
in your ability to succeed
and is expressed in many ways.
They way we look, the way we act and speak,
the manner in which we do things.
Our choice of motor vehicle and home,
and definitely our choice of clothing, denotes our level of confidence.
Some are quietly confident, not needing to impress.
Others can be more expressive.
Our body language and Posture says a lot about our
Confidence in the way we sit and stand,
our carriage whilst walking and our facial expression.
Smiling is a confidence tool.
The tone and volume of our Voice and a strong
Handshake denotes confidence.
Confidence is also expressed subconsciously and impressed on others.
Confidence says a lot about who we are and who we think we are.
If we don't have a high opinion of ourself, how can anyone else?
Confidence may just be a case of changing our mind
to change our habit and be who we are, or would like to be.
Gradually changing our opinion to a more positive belief and standing tall,
can become a natural way of being.
Confidence is having that inner resolve
that assures others that we know who we are and
accept ourselves the way we are, loving ourselves and therefore others.
Certain Colours can help us to feel more confident
Black is powerful, blue is Confident, purple regal.
Some who choose to be more Confident, but are not quite there yet,
choose to "fake it 'till they make it"
thus giving others an impression of their Confidence.

Confidence

Contemplate
the meaning
and aspects
of "Confidence"
in relation to the self
and life generally.
The affirmation and
Visualisation
for "Confidence"
should be used daily
and affirmed audibly
to empower the words
and the meaning
of "Confidence".
The verses have been added
for your enjoyment.

Confidence

Confidence says a lot about who we are
and who we think we are.
If we don't have a high opinion of ourself,
how can anyone else?
Confidence may just be a case of changing our mind,
to change our habit and be who we are,
or would like to be.
Gradually changing our opinion
to be of a more positive belief and standing tall
can become a natural way of being.
Confidence is having that inner resolve,
that assures others that we know who we are and
accept ourselves the way we are,
striving to be the best version of who we are,
loving ourselves and therefore others.
Certain colours can help us to feel more confident.
Black is powerful, blue is confident, purple is regal.
Some who choose to be more confident but are not quiet there yet,
can choose to "fake it till they make it"
thus giving others an impression of a confident sate.

Self Acceptance

Having
Self Acceptance
of who we are
through love of self,
we present to the world
as the individual we are.
Truly unique in every way.
We are all here
for a specific purpose
and have chosen to come in the
form we are in.
Be that dark skinned,
light skinned, red haired,
short or tall.
Therefore we can be self accepting of who we are,
warts and all.
Accepting that we all have something
we might wish to change,
is essential to achieving
confidence.
Talent, beauty, success,prosperity and fame
are "perceived"
and we all have them
in our own way.
Confidence is a learned attribute.
Confidence is having
Self Acceptance,
loving ourself.
with
Self-Acceptance and self-love,
We can project Confidence and self assuredness at all times.

Affirmation

Each day
in every way
I have
Self Acceptance.
No matter how I look
How I feel
How life is treating me
I have
Self Acceptance
because I know
I am truly unique.
I focus
on my
special features
and my
special talents
and I know there is
no-one like me
I accept myself as a
unique spirit and unit
of the whole of all
that is in
this Universe.
I am confident.
I have
Self Acceptance.

Visualisation

With closed eyes and a tranquil mind
Imagine your Self Acceptance
for all to see.
Visualise your Self Acceptance
and view and appreciate
every aspect of yourself.
Visualise your mind, your emotions,
and your spirit or
soul, and bath each aspect
in your Self Acceptance.

Individuality

Individuality is a specific personality,
character or characteristic that
distinguishes one person from another.
Confidence is being
Individual.
Standing out from the crowd.
Expressing our uniqueness
Individually.
Dressing to express how we feel
and who we are.
Seeking like people and events
to nurture our
Individuality.
Our home reflects our
Individuality in our choice of colour
and décor.
Our motor vehicle expresses our
Individuality
by its design and colour
Our chosen career also expresses our
Individuality.

Affirmation

Each day
in every way,
I acknowledge
that I am
Individual.
No other is as I am.
I am unique.
I give thanks for my
Body as my temple,
My mind as my Creator
My emotions as
my regulator.
My Spirit as my guide
I am
Individual.

Visualisation

With closed eyes and a tranquil mind –
Imagine your Individuality for all to see:
Visualise every aspect of your
Individuality,
What sets you apart from everyone else.
What makes you unique.
Focus on your
Individuality
and give thanks for the
uniqueness that is you.

Independence

Independence is freedom from
dependence on
or control by another person,
state or organisation
Confidence is being
Independent.
Being self sufficient
in every way.
Not relying on others
unnecessarily.
Being financially
Independent gives us
Control over our lives,
Being emotionally and
Physically
Independent
Represents total freedom.
Striving for
Independence.
Is our personal responsibility
In life as we choose to live in
Inter or codependency,
and not dependent on others.
Independence
sets us apart.

Affirmation

Each day
in every way,
I am
Independent.
I work to be
Independent.
I live to be
Independent
When I meet my friends and
partner in life, they are
Independent.
Although I welcome assistance
when I require it,
I am essentially
Independent
and self sufficient in my life.
I am
Independent.

Visualisation

With closed eyes and a tranquil mind –
Imagine your Independence
for all to see:
See yourself as an Independent,
individual, functioning
autonomously where necessary.
Visualise yourself as self sufficient
in every way,
not relying on others,
but being
Independent.

Poise

Poise is a calm, self assured
dignity especially when
dealing with social situations.
Confidence is having
Poise.
No matter what is happening
around us
we can stay in control with grace and
Poise.
No matter what is said or acted,
we may choose
to not react or respond,
but to simply stay calm.
Poise is the tool of the elegant
and finely bread woman
and men of history and the world.
Those who have
Confidence in themselves
and are not, and do not live at
The whim of the world
they have
Poise.

Affirmation

Each day
in every way
I am
Poised.
In any given situation.
In being
Poised,
I learn
to have confidence
I am
Poised.

Visualisation

With closed eyes and a tranquil mind –
Imagine your
Poise for all to see:
Visualise yourself in social or
work situations, acting with
Poise.
See yourself with perfect posture,
smiling charmingly,
thinking before you speak,
listening intently to others,
being
Poised.

Calm

Being calm is being without
anxiety
or strong emotion.
Confidence is staying
Calm
no matter what
is happening in our life.
When those around us
loose control,
breath deeply and remain
Calm
knowing that this
will support our
confidence.
Confident people need not
Submit unnecessarily to
Emotion, they stay
Calm.

Affirmation

Each day
in every way
I am
Calm .
Through my deep
breathing
and my inner resolve
to build my confidence
I stay
Calm.
Staying
Calm
Allows me to
stay in control.
I am
Calm.

Visualisation

With closed eyes and a tranquil mind –
Imagine your
Calm for all to see:
Calmness is a learned skill
of breathing deeply,
Visualise yourself staying centred,
thinking considerately
prior to speaking and
remaining
Calm.

.

Inner Peace

Inner Peace is a
state of calm
devoid of anxiety.
Confidence is having
Inner Peace.
In accepting totally
who we are.
We recognise our positive
and negative traits and
focus on developing
ourselves more positively with
Inner Peace.
If at any time we feel
we are not coping in a situation,
we can go to a quiet place
and re-establish our
Inner Peace.
Our Inner Peace
radiates from
a space deep within our soul
and supports us in times of
external stress.
Focusing on our
Inner Peace at any time
brings us back to a state of ability to function
under all conditions and challenges
life may present.

Affirmation

Each day
in every way
I become more confident
with
Inner Peace
as I understand who I am
and the role I play in the
great game of life.
I have control of my
thoughts and emotions.
As I create what I need
in my life with love,
trust and faith
in myself and all that is.
I have
Inner Peace.

Visualisation

With closed eyes and a tranquil mind –
Imagine your Inner Peace for all to see:
Visualise yourself having
Inner Peace at all times.
See yourself as a person with
Inner Peace as a part of your being.
No matter what is happening around you,
you are unaffected with
Inner Peace.

.

Posture

Good Posture is the way in
which somebody
carries his or her body,
especially when standing,
good posture can therefore
denote a level of Confidence.
Standing tall and erect,
with shoulders held down,
and head held high, can assist
in making a person feel
Confident and therefore
appear Confident
with good posture.

Affirmation

Each day in every way
I am aware of my Posture.
I know that my
Posture indicates my
Confidence.
Therefore at all times
I stand and sit tall
aware of my Posture.

Visualisation

With closed eyes and a tranquil mind –
Imagine your
Posture for all to see
Visualise your Posture as perfect,
straight and strong.
See yourself standing tall at all times
in complete Confidence of who you are
with good posture.

.

Grace

A person of Grace shows tact,
kindness, politeness and elegance
in any situation.
Grace lends itself to an air
of Confidence in any person.
Great leaders in all areas of life
have and show Grace at all times.

Affirmation

Each day in every way
I have Grace.
In all circumstances
I am Gracious.
No matter the stress
or challenge
I stand with
Grace.

Visualisation

With closed eyes and a tranquil mind –
Imagine your Grace for all
to see and experience.
Visualise yourself with a Graceful
demeanour as you approach life.
See yourself grateful and giving to all
you encounter on your path
with Confidence and
Grace.

Dress

A Confident person wears clothing
of a particular type,
worn in a particular way,
appropriate to a particular occasion.
Colour and style add impact to ones stye of dress.
Black and red are power colours for corporate occasion.
Tailored lines allow the person to shine
without distraction of too much colour, print or elaborate design.
Dignified clothing is usually the
choice for corporate apparel
Fun colours and design for casual occasions
and elegant shimmers in the evening as well.
Dress for the event.

Affirmation

Each day in every way
I Dress for the occasion
I choose my style and
colours to fit the situation.
I express myself through my
choice of clothing and
Dress.

Visualisation

With closed eyes and a tranquil mind –
Imagine your
Dress for all to see
Visualise yourself
Dressed for Confidence.
See yourself in strongly defined
style and power colours in your
personal choice of Dress.

Smile

Smiling is sign of happiness,
pleasure, self-contentment,
and joy and
always endears the
person to others.
Smiling is also a
sign of Confidence,
so Smile and appear to
be so.

Affirmation

Each day in every way
I Smile.
I Smile at all I encounter
throughout the day.
I know that when I
Smile at another person,
my Smile
may allow the other person to feel better.
Smiles don't cost anything
and
they use less muscles than
frowning
so I Smile.

Visualisation

With closed eyes and a tranquil mind –
Imagine your Smile for all to see.
Visualise yourself
Smiling at each encounter.
See others Smiling back at you
as the ripple
in the pond spreading Smiles to all.
See yourself more Confident as your
Smile becomes a part of
your daily presentation and expression
Smile.

Charm

.
A Charming person has the power
to delight or attract people.
Usually a "people" person.
A Charming person loves social interaction
and is very keen and able to please.
Charming people have an abundance of
Confidence as they usually
believe in themselves
and therefore focus on others,
with Charm.

Affirmation

Each day in every way,
I am Charming
I enjoy the company of others
and know that
Charm attracts people
therefore I am
Charming.

Visualisation

Visualise yourself as Charming
Imagine yourself attracting those you
would like to have in your life.
See yourself as the
centre of attention
at social functions as
people warm to you
and love to be around you,
because you are
Charming.

Handshake

A Handshake is a gesture
of gripping and shaking
another person's hand as a
greeting or farewell
or to seal an agreement.
A firm Handshake is an indication of
Confidence and a solid character.
Matching the other's
Handshake can be a mark of
respect and can indicate unison.
Make your Handshake
warm and embracing
to make a positive impression.

Affirmation

Each day in every way
I greet people with a warm,
firm Handshake.
I know that I will make a better
impression with my
Handshake when I am focused
on expressing myself
in a positive manner
through my
Handshake.

Visualisation

With closed eyes and a tranquil mind –
Imagine your firm
Handshake for all to experience
Visualise yourself stepping forward,
smiling and
presenting a firm Handshake
when meeting someone for the first time.
See yourself maintaining a firm Handshake
but also matching the Handshake of the recipient,
so as not to appear overbearing to a gentle,
or weak to a very strong person.
Imagine your
Handshake expressing your character
with Confidence.

Eye Contact

The act of looking directly into the eyes of
another is very important
to the Confident person.
Eye contact denotes Confidence,
honesty, directness and openness and
is essential to a Confident person.
Always maintain
Eye Contact
to appear Confident.

Affirmation

Each day in every way
I make Eye Contact
with those I encounter
I know that I am assessed
by my Eye Contact as a
direct and honest person.
Therefore I maintain
Eye Contact
at all times.

Visualisation

Visualise yourself maintaining
Eye Contact
during your initial
encounter with a person,
your
handshake and
continued conversation.
The person will then see
you as honest, direct
and confident
with maintained
eye contact.

Voice

Voice is the sound produced
by using the vocal chords in speech
and singing as a medium
of communication.
A Confident person has a voice
that is well modulated
and that person
speaks slowly and clearly.

Affirmation

Each day in every way,
I am aware of my Voice.
I consider my Voice
as well modulated.
I express my concerns,
desires, opinions and
personal communication
through my Voice when I speak.
Therefore I am very
aware of the
impression my
Voice makes
when I speak.

Visualisation

With closed eyes and a tranquil mind –
Imagine your
Voice expressing who you are
and what you wish to convey
for others to experience.
Visualise yourself
speaking with a well-modulated tone.
See yourself speaking
slowly as you deliver
your message
with a Confident voice.

Confidence Verse

As I awaken each morning and stretch
I contemplate what I do best
What I enjoy about myself
What I can do to improve my test In life.

Reflecting on my tapestry
I release what may be hindering me.
The negative patterns of the past
The excess baggage that I cart
Around with me needlessly.

Now released through thought and deed
Replaced with love and faith in need
To be all than I am and all I can be
Experiencing my life now in harmony.

Confidence is a state of mind
Nowhere in a tablet will we find
Confidence to be taken at will
Confidence labelled on the side of a pill.

Of who you are in body, mind and spirt,
Accept who you are, have pride and love it.
We are who we are, in essence we know
We have choice to change and grow.

Into more, of what we would like to be,
stronger decisive, committed and free.
From the ravages of fear, that may hold us back
The negative thoughts that may keep us off track.

Confidence is a learned thing an art –a skill
Having faith in self a skill achieved at will
In pride of appearance and personal fitness
Take a look in a mirror and bare the witness.

Using Confidence as a daily skill
One to be applied, on call, at will
To have faith in ourselves, we are unique
Children of the Universe, and as we speak.

So we create what we will achieve
What we want for ourselves, what we believe
We as the creator, of our domain
Confidence an aspect, life just a game.

So don't take it seriously, life is to enjoy
Confidence a support, as just one more toy
To be played with, on this stage of life
enjoy the game in fun, with less strife.

Confidence, is a state of mind
Believe in your self and you will find
Other's in turn will believe in you
Believe in the truth, the truth to be true.

Act with Confidence.

Communication Verse

What to say and how to say it
Trained from birth to talk, albeit
Contrived ,to please those who hear
The trainers of life, those so dear.

We want to please, come what may
Always, the right things to say
Chosen words, to suite the need
Learned response, to suit the deed.

"Out of the mouths of babes" they cry
Truth projected, then to ask why
We choose to edit, and manipulate
Words so pure, truth so great.

Do we choose to speak then, from the heart
Intended truth, needed to impart
Or choose to conform, to social standard
Otherwise a rebel, then to be branded.

Non conformist, troublemaker, named
Speaking the truth, the only blame
What punishment, for this vocal crime
To live with lies then, for the rest of time.

Or speak the truth, and pay the price
Who are you, or just be nice
Communication, always a choice
Time to reflect, the power of voice.

teen AMBITION guide

by LYNN MERRIN

Ambition

This book is designed
to encourage the reader
to contemplate
the meaning
and aspects
of
Ambition
in relation to the self
and Life generally.
The Affirmation and Visualisation
for
Ambition
can be used daily
and affirmed audibly
to empower the words
and the meaning
of
Ambition.
The book and contents
have been charged
with the universal energy
Of Reiki
The verse has been added
For your enjoyment.

Looking at the various aspects
of expression of Ambition
we consider the following;

Vision	determining what our purpose and goal is
Focus	having a goal and keeping our eye on it
Drive	the will and determination to push through
Determination	the will to achieve our goals no matter what
Will	the inner resolve to carry out our mission
Need	to have the success and all it represents
Vitality	inner resource and energy
Trust	in self and all that is
Faith	that all is what it should be
Desire	the desire to succeed
Thought	taking the time to think things through thoroughly
Plan	planning each and every step to take
Ideas	formulating ideas and actioning them
Motivation	having the get up and go to get things done
Goals	setting realistic goals and achieving them
Action	taking the necessary action to drive the goals
Perseverance	not giving up when times get tough
Ethics	having the correct moral code to succeed
Respect	showing respect to all involved on the way
Co-operation	working as a team to get things done
Delegation	relinquishing control where necessary

Ambition

Is having a Vision.
Setting our sights on our goal and
not being deterred
no matter what obstacles present.
Holding the Vision with trust and faith.
Actioning our ideas.
Having the motivation, determination,
perseverance and trust
that our goals and dreams will be achieved.
Never giving up no matter what.
Remaining focused at all times.
Actioning our plans.
Staying open to new ideas and
making corrections along the way.
Remembering that to err is human.
Including our colleagues in our success
Always maintaining our moral code
Remembering the less fortunate
and tithing 10% of our income
Is desirable and, it is said,
returns ten fold
A motto is
"Do It Now".

Affirmation

Each day in every way
I am
Ambitious.
I strive to achieve.
I am motivated.
I believe I can achieve my goals.
I action my ideas.
I am focused,
determined and driven.
My mind is focused
at all times on success.
No matter what is happening in my life,
I hold the Vision in my mind
knowing that it will,
by Universal Law, manifest.
I am
Ambitious.

Visualisation

With closed eyes and
a tranquil mind,
Imagine your Ambition
for all to see:
See yourself charged
with energy
to achieve your goals.
Visualise your goals.
See them coming to fruition.
See the outcome in your mind,
that is where it begins.
See your self celebrating your
Ambitious success.

Vision

Ambition
Is having a Vision.
A vision should be held in mind
at all times.
Undeterred, focus on your Vision.
As an archer focuses on his target
drive your arrow home to the bullseye
and your Vision is realised.
Never lose sight of your Vision
Your Vision is my dream,
your goal and your purpose.

Affirmation

Each and every day
I focus on my
Vision.
As a camera to a screen
My mind holds my
Vision
and projects it onto the screen
of my existence.
I have a
Vision.

Visualisation

With closed eyes and a
tranquil mind
Imagine your Vision
complete.
Focus on your Vision in detail.
See the outcome.
Visualise the resulting
rewards of your Vision.
See yourself celebrating
your Vision coming to fruition.

Focus

Is
Focusing on goals
and the task at hand.
Focusing no matter what
may arise as a distraction.
Focus is maintained
at all times.
Through good and bad days,
Focus is held as a discipline,
to realise dreams
and ambitions,
through
Focus.

Affirmation

Each day
in every way,
I Focus
on my goal.
I know that while I hold
my vision in mind,
affirming the outcome
and
Focus,
my goal will be realised.
I know that energy flows
where my attention goes,
so my attention is on my goal.
I am
Focused.

Visualisation

With closed eyes and
a tranquil mind
Imagine yourself
Focusing on your ambition.
See yourself becoming that
Ambitious person.
See yourself successful
in every way.
Visualise yourself totally
Focused on
whatever you are doing
at any time.
See yourself as a
Focused person
at all times.

Drive

Drive, can be to provide
momentum toward the
successful operation
or functioning
of something.

Ambition Is having the
Drive
to achieve your goals.
To be not only mentally
Driven
but to be physically,
emotionally and
spiritually
Driven
in support of your
Drive to achieve
all that you want, need
and desire in life.

Affirmation

Each day
in every way
I have the
Drive
to succeed.
I am disciplined
mentally, physically
and emotionally,
in support
of my Drive.
I am
Driven
to succeed.

I have Drive.

Visualisation

With closed eyes and
a tranquil mind,
Imagine your
Drive for all to see:
Visualise yourself
Driven to success.
Imagine your determination
and persistence to succeed.
Visualise your Drive
taking you to whatever
level you choose to
achieve in life.

Determination

Determination is
firmness of purpose,
will or intention.
Ambition
Is having the
Determination
to succeed.
The Determination
to continue
when things get tough.
The Determination
to overcome every obstacle
on our path
The Determination
to reach our goals.

Affirmation

Each day
In every way,
I am
Determined.
I am Determined
to meet my goals,
regardless
of what challenges and
obstacles
may present
on my path.
I just keep on keeping on,
until I reach my goal.
I am
Determined.

Visualisation

With closed eyes and
a tranquil mind,
Imagine your
Determination
increasing:
Visualise yourself with
the necessary
Determination
to get you to the top of
your profession,
or chosen role in life.
See yourself at the top,
celebrating your
Determination and
success.

Will

Will is that part of the mind that
consciously decides things.
Ambition Is having
the Will
to succeed and
achieve our goals in life.
We need to have a deep
need to achieve.
and our
Will
will see us through,
no matter what
deterrents we may face.
With due consideration,
our Will drives our
Ambition.

Affirmation

Each day
in every way,
I have the
Will
to succeed.
My Will
is deeply rooted
in my psyche
and will support me
throughout my life.
I have strong
Will.

Visualisation

With closed eyes and
a tranquil mind,
Imagine your Will
increasing:
Visualise and feel
the power of your Will.
See your Will
driving you
to persist and
never give in.
Visualise and you
Will succeed.

Need

Need is used to indicate
that something is required,
in order to have
success or achieve something.
Ambition
Is having the
Need
to achieve, the things
we want to have
in our life.
Without a
Need,
There is no
Need
to achieve.

Affirmation

Each day
in every way,
I assess my
Need
to achieve,
being aware that my
Needs
are not necessarily
material.
I balance my physical,
mental,
emotional and
spiritual needs,
considering that family and
health are my priority.
I have the
Need
to achieve.

Visualisation

With closed eyes and a
tranquil mind,
Imagine your
Need to be successful:
Visualise the
outcome and the happiness
you will experience.
Imagine the comforts you may provide
with your ambition.
Visualise the things or outcome
you Need.
See yourself enjoying the things you
Need to have in your life.

Vitality

Vitality is abundant physical
and mental energy,
usually combined with a
wholehearted and joyous approach
to situations and activities.
Ambition Is having the Vitality
to succeed in our life.
The energy
to meet the demands.
The Vibrancy
to support our activities.
To be aware of the
quality of food we ingest,
The exercise
we engage in each day.
The quality of air we breath,
The quality of our thoughts
and feelings,
to ensure the level
of our
Vitality
Is maintained at all times.

Affirmation

Each day
in every way
I am
Vital.
The energy of the universe
flows through me,
to touch all I meet.
I nurture my body,
my mind and
my spirit,
with positive in-put.
I am
Vital.

Visualisation

With closed eyes and a
tranquil mind,
Imagine yourself as a
Vital person
See your Vitality sparkling
through your eyes
Evident in your enthusiasm.
See yourself energised,
with your
Vitality
driving your
Ambition.

Trust

Trust is
confidence in and
reliance on good
qualities,
especially fairness,
truth,
honour, or ability.
Ambition is having
Trust
in ourself,
our colleagues
and the Universe,
That our vision,
focus and ability
is true for us.
That we will succeed
in this world of
challenges
and obstacles,
we need to
Trust.

Affirmation

Each day
in every way,
I Trust.
I Trust
myself and
the Universe
in the plan of my life.
I Trust that I am
supported and loved
in my quest.
I Trust.

Visualisation

With closed eyes and a
tranquil mind,
Imagine your Trust for all
to see and experience.
Visualise yourself being
Trusting in each
encounter with others.
Visualise your intuition
guiding you in that
Trust
and enjoy the openness, with
confidence in your
Ambition.

Faith

Faith is a belief in,
devotion to, or trust in
somebody,
especially without
logical proof.
Ambition Is having
Faith
that all is happening
as it should be in our life.
with Faith,
we, as the creator of our
existence,
are being guided along our path
by the Universal energy of love,
with Faith,
As surely as the sun rises each day,
we should have Faith
that our guided life
is unfolding as it should.

Affirmation

Each day
in every way
I have
Faith.
I know that I am
in control of my destiny
That I can change my life
when I need to.
I know that I am supported
by the Universe
at all times,
even when things
may seem
not to be going my way,
as anticipated
I have
Faith.

Visualisation

With closed eyes and a
tranquil mind,
Imagine your
Faith for all to see.
Visualise
yourself having
Faith
and not fear,
as you start
each day.
See your
Faith giving you
Confidence.

Desire

Ambition Is having the
Desire
To achieve our
dreams.
Without Desire,
our dreams
are just that,
Dreams.
Desire
is the catalyst
for things
to happen.
The motivational
magic,
is Desire.

Affirmation

Desire
Each day
in every day
I have the
Desire
to achieve
my dreams.
I feel the
Desire
deep in my
Soul.
I
Desire.

Visualisation

With closed eyes and
a tranquil mind,
Imagine your Desire:
Without Desire,
the dream sleeps,
to Visualise your
Desire burning
within you,
to project your
dreams
to reality.

Thoughts and Ideas

Thoughts and ideas
Are required for
Ambition
to be achieved
as part of the formula.
Thoughtful Ideas
project us forward,
on our path of success.
With an open mind,
Thoughts and Ideas
can be
inspired.

Affirmation

Each day
in every way,
I keep an open mind.
My
Thoughts and Ideas
are inspired.
As I focus on my
ambition,
I have Thoughtful
Ideas
I am
Thoughtful.

Visualisation

With closed eyes and
a tranquil mind,
Visualise your Thoughts and Ideas.
Thoughts are energy
and manifest into form, so
Ideas are inspiration,
manifest, for you to action.
See your Ideas becoming a reality,
woven into the fabric of
your ambitious success.
Carefully visualise what your
Thoughts and Ideas
can create,
in your ambition to succeed.

Action

Ambition requires
considered Action.
Action
is required,
to project our
Ideas and goals
into being.
Without
Action,
We have only ideas
and dreams
That go nowhere.

Affirmation

Each day
in every way
I
Action
my thoughts and ideas.
I know that without
Action,
Nothing
will materialise.
I Action.

Visualisation

With closed eyes and a
tranquil mind,
Visualise yourself
Actioning
your goals,
thoughts, ideas
and dreams.
Once the idea has
been born,
it require
Action to manifest
See yourself in Action,
moving your intentions
forward toward
your
ambitious goals.

Ethics

Ethics is a system of moral
principles governing
the appropriate
conduct for any individual,
or group.
Ambition requires
Ethics
to become successful.
Many have failed on the
climb to the top,
through lacking
Ethics.
To sustain our journey
at all times,
Honesty,
Reliability, Respect,
Truth, Loyalty
and all moral principles
should be applied,
as Ethics.

Affirmation

Each day
in every way
I am
Ethical.
I acknowledge
that without
Ethics,
I have no principles
and will not be
ultimately
successful.
I am
Ethical.

Visualisation

With closed eyes and
a tranquil mind,
Visualise yourself
with sound Ethics.
See yourself enjoying
success in an
Ethical environment,
as an Ethical person,
consciously acting in an
Ethical manner
at all times,
for assured success.

Cooperation

To work or act together,
to achieve a common aim.
Ambition requires
Cooperation.
Without
Cooperation,
we may find ourself
at the top of the ladder
alone.
Cooperation takes the
team with us to the top,
where all can benefit in
Cooperation.

Affirmation

Each day
in every day,
I choose to
Cooperate.
I know that working
as a team,
will benefit,
myself and
my colleagues.
I
Cooperate.

Visualisation

With closed eyes and
a tranquil mind,
Visualise yourself in
an environment of
Co-operation.
See yourself
Co-operating
with others,
as they
Co-operate with you.
Visualise your success in
Co-operation
on each and
every occasion.

Delegation

Delegation is the giving
of some power, responsibilty or
work to somebody else.
Ambition requires
Delegation.
Without
Delegation
we are in control, but
our workload is heavy
and our colleagues
under realised.
Delegation,
allows more time
for us to supervise
and enjoy freer time
for ourselves
so Delegate.

Affirmation

Each day
in every way
I
Delegate.
I realise that without
Delegating,
I am bound to
over-work
I
Delegate.

Visualisation

With closed eyes and
a tranquil mind,
Visualise yourself
Delegating
to others.
See yourself using
leverage
to succeed,
by trusting and
Delegating
to others.

Ambition Verse

Striving through life, on our way to the top
We sometimes forget, what we should not
Those who may not be, as fortunate as we
Those who don't have, the opportunities to be.

All they could be, in this challenging world
Or even who they really are, we are told.
So as we strive on our pathway, to the top.
Let us pause and take a short time to stop

and consider those, less fortunate than we.
Those who may still have, the chance to be.
All they can be, in this world of plenty.
In this world of opportunity and beauty.

Give from the heart, when you see a chance.
Then your life as well could be enhanced.
When you think to give, to someone in need.
The kindness will return ten fold in deed.

For what we give out, we in turn receive.
Consider this, when you strive to achieve
A life of harmony, happiness, wisdom and wealth.
Companionship, freedom, friendship and health.

As we strive to achieve, all we can be.
Learning, working, climbing, we see.
The goal ahead, the target, the aim.
The path to follow, to claim our fame.

While we have Ambition, others may not.
So let us remember, those others forgot.
Let our ambition always, be shared with another.
So they in turn, may help their brother.

When they have remembered, to follow their dream.
Awaken from the slumber, the realisation unseen.
To awaken their Ambition, to be all they can be.
To realise their potential, and strive to see

a way out of the darkness and into the light.
To recover the confidence and courage to fight.
For the right to be present and enjoy each day.
To grow in strength, in every way.

Ambition, is a great tool, on the road through life.
Fuel for the passage, accelleration, cutting knife.
Or just determination, to be the best we can be.
To help those who ask, those who can't see.

As clearly as we, in a passageway dark.
Coming into the light, can often be stark.
Realisation, of what has been lost.
In time, in space, in financial cost.

Ambition helps us to improve our state.
Help someone on their way, help a mate.
To make a better world, better life, better place.
For each of us to experience, our experience, in grace.

Share your Ambition

© Lynn Merrin 2024

teen LOVE guide

by LYNN MERRIN

Introduction

Love is an inspiring book designed to
assist you to make positive change in your life.

Take a personal journey of consideration,
beyond the physical,
to further understand the subconscious
mind from a metaphysical viewpoint.

Confidence is the first of four motivational guides,
complete with inspiring verses,
daily affirmations and creative visualisations.
These verses are charged with Reiki energy to enhance
these personally empowering processes.

Love

This book is designed
to encourage the reader
to contemplate
the meaning
and aspects
of "Love"
in relation to the self
and life generally.
the Affirmation and Visualisation
for "Love"
should be used daily
and affirmed audibly
to empower the words
and the meaning
of Love.
The verse has been added
for your enjoyment.
The book and contents
have been charged
with the Universal energy
of Reiki.

Looking at the various aspects of expression of love consider the following;

Love	is unconditional. An energy with no boundaries
Care	being there for others with love
Consideration	putting others first with a loving heart
Appreciation	being grateful for what we have with love
Admiration	commending others on achievements
Recognition	acknowledging positive effort
Listening	to what others/nature has to say
Hearing	what others/nature has to express
Seeing	from the heart, what really is – the truth
Speaking	the truth from the heart
Nurturing	self and others in love
Faith	belief in the creation of the positive energy of all things including love
Accepting	the things I cannot change etc
Trust	in self and universe with love
Presence	being available on every level
Dignity	allowing others their dignity
Being	I am

Love

Much has been written about love throughout the ages
and, as an intangible form,
love is sometimes difficult to define.
The ancient Hawaiian culture knows "All is love".
As night and day, dark and light,
Yin and Yang, good and bad,
we can choose to be "in love"
Love is unconditional.
It just is
Love is energy with no boundaries,
no conditions and it's there for all, all the time!
All we need to do is embrace it,
use it as part of our daily way of life.
A difficult task?
Sometimes!
But, when we give love,
We are bound to receive love.
if we don't,
perhaps we have awakened a small spark
within the recipient anyway.
People and animals come alive when they are given love.
as energy matching their soul, they are fed and nurtured,
their battery charged so to speak.
It is said that energy surrounds all matter and that matter is
simply energy vibrating at a denser rate.
If love is energy, how would this energy effect
the dense matter of our physical body?
How many orphaned babies died
when they were not touched in Romania?
How many people ultimately
die after they loose their loved one?
Love is essential to our very existence
and should be revered accordingly.

—

Affirmation

Each day, in every way,
Love fills my life.
With every breath,
Love fills every cell
of my Body,
my Mind and my Spirit.
Love fills every part of my life.
Love is Loving myself
as I Love others.
Each and every
thing I do is
in Love.
I am a more
Loving person
knowing that as
I fill my own cup,
I give Love
to all I encounter
I Love.

Visualisation

With closed eyes and a tranquil mind
Imagine yourself in a state
of Love.
Allow Love to wash over you.
Visualise Love permeating
every cell in your body.
See Love emanating from you
at all times.
Allow Love to be present
in every word you speak.
Visualise Love
in everything you see.

Care

To Care is to feel affection,
love and concern for someone.
Love is
Caring for others
when they are feeling down
physically, mentally, emotionally
or spiritually.
Being there and supporting
them as they find their own way back
to a more positive state.
Love is
Caring for self first.
To be better equipped
to be of service to others.
As the cup fills –
so it spills over to others.
How can we Care for and love another
If we can't Care for
and give love to ourselves?

Affirmation

Each day
in every way
I Care.
I Care
for myself,
for my loved ones
and all I encounter
throughout the day.
I Care
for the environment
and all living things
I Care.

Visualisation

With closed eyes and a tranquil mind –
Imagine being more Caring:
Caring for yourself and filling your cup first
to enable you to care for others.
Caring for family
regardless of the circumstance.
Having empathy and caring for those less fortunate.
Caring for the environment and making
the necessary changes to support it.
Being Caring will become automatic
when you imagine,
then become more caring.
This will be returned to you as the
action and reaction of physics.

Consideration

Consideration is thoughtful
concern for
or sensitivity toward the
feelings of others.
Love is
Considering
others and their needs
as our own.
We remember
that when we treat
others as
we would be treated,
we get back
what we put out.
With every thought
and action,
we are creating
our own destiny.
Therefore we
consider the feelings,
the rights
and spirit
of all we encounter.

Affirmation

Each day
in every way
I am
Considerate
of others.
I know that
whatever I give out,
will come back to me.
Therefore,
I am conscious
of my every thought,
deed and word.
I am
Considerate.

Visualisation

With closed eyes and a tranquil mind –
Imagine Considering
all you encounter.
Thinking prior to speaking
Considering the needs of others
at all times.
Consdiering each action before taken
and the results of activities,
prior to engaging them.
When Considering with your mind,
prior to action,
you become more Considerate
This will in turn,
return to you from others.

Appreciation

Appreciation is the full understanding
and importance of something.
Love is
Appreciating
and
being happy with
what we have.
The grass isn't always
greener on
the other side.
Life can be
an illusion.
So,
when we awaken
each morning,
give thanks
for what we have.
No matter what it is
there is always
someone with less.
Also remember that
what we focus on,
we get more of,
so, we focus on plenty,
not lack in our life
with
Appreciation.

Affirmation

Each day in every way
I give thanks
and
Appreciate.
I am grateful
for what
I have in my life.
As I focus on
Appreciating
what I have,
it magnifies and
the focus on lack,
leaves my life
I Appreciate.

Visualisation

With closed eyes and a tranquil mind –
Imagine your Appreciation of the
good things that occur in your life:
The wonderful people who share
their time and energy with you.
Your family and friends.
The house you live in.
The bed that gives you a good nights sleep.
The food you eat to nourish you body.
The transport you enjoy.
The work you love to be paid to do.
The relaxation activities you enjoy participating in.
The pets you love, that love you.
The men and women who have sacrificed
to give the freedom to live in democracy.
The fresh air you breathe.
The fresh water you drink.
Appreciation for the things we enjoy
will flow on to others and return to you.

Admiration

Admiration is a feeling of pleasure
and approval and, often wonder.
Love is
Admiring
others.
Focusing on the good,
the well done, the effort made.
Therefore,
take any opportunity
to Admire
and commend others.
For their achievements
no matter how small.
Acknowledge
that a child
will grow tall and strong
if his efforts
and achievements
are rewarded and
Admired.
Remember that
charity begins at home
and give yourself
a pat on the back
for your
Achievements
too!

Affirmation

Each day in every way
I Admire.
The special attributes
of others and myself.
I take
the time to stop,
appreciate
and Admire
the wonder
of all that it is.
Knowing
that there is
beauty in all
and
what I focus on,
I get more
of in my life.
I
Admire
the beauty
in all living things.
I Admire.

Visualisation

With closed eyes and a tranquil mind –
Imagine your Admiration for all you see.
Visualise a beautiful garden, lovingly created
Nature's majesty reflected in a beach,
mountain, valley, river, lake, sky
See a majestic building,
the result of many ideas and skills.
A mother caring for her young
with dedication and love.
A worker hard at their job,
enjoying their role creating their living.
An animal, loyally dedicated to his master.
See the perfection in all things and
Admire the many aspects of all that is.

Recognition

Recognition
is appreciation
or fame
earned by achievement.
Love is
Recognising
the goodness,
the talent, the skills,
the beauty in others
as well as ourself.
As every day
has light as well as dark,
focus on
Recognising
the "light" in others
and ourself
and let it grow.
Even those who appear
to have fallen by the wayside
have light in their soul.
Recognise
this,
so that it may grow
within them also.

Affirmation

Each day
in every way
I
Recognise
the goodness
in all
as well as myself.
I
Recognise
that
when I focus on good,
I will get
more goodness
in my life.
I
Recognise.

Visualisation

With closed eyes and a tranquil mind –
Imagine yourself
Recognising
Signs and signals that guide your life.
Recognising what is good for you
and what is not.
Be prepared to
Recognise your fate each day
through the numerous
signs that present in life
Recognise.

Listening

Listening is to concentrate
on hearing somebody
or something.
Love is
Listening.
We are all teachers
as well as students.
Everyone
has something to say.
Love is
Listening
with an open heart and
without judgement,
to what others
have to say.
Love is
Listening
to the sounds of nature
and also to ourself,
as our"inner voice"
is there to guide us
when we
Listen.

Affirmation

Each day
in every way
I
Listen.
To the sounds of nature,
the words of others
and my intuition.
I draw from
what I have heard.
What my
intuition tells me
is true for me.
I
Listen.

Visualisation

With closed eyes and a tranquil mind –
Imagine yourself
Listening clearly.
Contemplate taking the time to Listen.
Listen intently to what is said.
Listening is a mark of respect and
often we hear what we need to learn
See yourself
Listening
with every part of your being.

Hearing

Hearing is a
opportunity
to be heard,
especially an opportunity
to state an opinion
or fact.
Love is
Hearing
what others say
not
filtering the words
to be what
we want to Hear.
Love is
Hearing
without fear, through
a pure heart,
with the
courage to Hear
the truth.
Love is
taking the time to
also Hear
the pure
sounds of nature.

Affirmation

Each day
in every way I
Hear
without fear.
I have an
open heart
and mind
to
Hear
what is presented
and know
what is true for me.
I Hear.

Visualisation

With closed eyes and a tranquil mind –
Imagine yourself
Hearing clearly.
Be aware of how your ear operates physically.
Imagine yourself
Hearing
with an open mind and a pure heart.
See yourself
Hearing what others say,
not what you think you hear.
Imagine enjoying the pure sounds of nature
Focusing on
Hearing what truly is each day in your life.

Speaking

Speaking is being capable of
communicating in an eloquent
or impressive way.
Love is
Speaking the truth
in a kind
and respectful manner.
Speaking
from the heart
with no judgement
or agenda.
Speaking
with clarity
and consideration
for the age and level of
comprehension of the recipient.
Speaking
in a manner
that allows the vibration,
the energy and
meaning of the words
to enhance the content,
and illuminate
the recipient.
Speak
From the heart.

Affirmation

Each day
in every way
I consciously
Speak
the truth.
I am aware
that
my words
are energy
and I
Speak
in a manner
that is loving.
I
consciously
Speak
the truth.

Visualisation

With closed eyes and a tranquil mind –
Imagine yourself Speaking clearly.
Imagine that what you intend
to say is verbalised exactly.
See yourself Speak with
courage and truth.
Imagine that your word
is your wand
to create your reality.

Nurturing

To nurture is to
encourage someone
or something to grow,
develop, thrive and
be successful.
Love is Nurturing others
as well as ourselves.
When
We take the time to
Nurture ourselves,
We "fill our cup"
to overflow to others
who need
Nurturing.
We remember
that charity
begins at home
so we
Nurture our body
with quality nutrition.
We Nurture our mind
with quality information.
We Nurture
our spirit
with quality of life.
Our Nurturing
extends
to all around us
especially the children,
animals, the elderly
and those in need.

Affirmation

Each day
in every way I Nurture.
I remember
to take the time
to do something
that I need to do
for myself.
When
I Nurture myself,
I have the energy
and heart
to be free to
Nurture
others with love.
I am
Nurturing.

Visualisation

With closed eyes and a tranquil mind –
Imagine yourself Nurturing.
Be aware of
Nurturing yourself.
Imagine yourself taking the time
for yourself in your busy schedule.
See yourself
Nurturing all who
come to you in times of need.
Imagine Nurturing,
being a part of your
psyche and daily habit
and you in turn, will be
Nurtured.

Faith

Faith is belief in,
devotion to,
or trust in somebody or
something especially
when there is no proof.
Love is
having Faith.
Day by day
as well as
in times of trouble,
for others
as well as ourselves.
Faith
is holding the vision
of a positive outcome
no matter what.
Having Faith
that everything
is happening as it should
and that each experience
and lesson,
is an opportunity
for growth.
Faith negates fear.
Fear is simply faith upside down.

Affirmation

Each day
in every way
I have
Faith.
I know that
when I hold
a positive vision
at all times,
what I am
focusing on
will become a reality.
I am the master
and creator
of my destiny.
I am
Faithful
I have
Faith.

Visualisation

With closed eyes and a tranquil mind,
Imagine being
Faithful in all you anticipate.
Put fear aside and have Faith.
See yourself having
Faith in yourself
and your abilities.
Imagine
Faith in the support
you receive from others.
See Faith in the Universe
supporting you on your path.
Visualise yourself
with
Faith in your heart at all times.

Accepting

Acceptance is the
willingness
to believe
that something is true.
Accepting self
and all,
is a necessary
challenge in life.
We are what we are
Things are what they are.
Acceptance,
brings peace
to a situation
we have no power over.
After all is said and done
that can be,
Acceptance is the next step
and ultimate freedom.

Affirmation

Each and every day
I Accept
what is presented to me
in a loving
and non-judgemental way.
I do my best
to stay in love
and goodness
and
Accept
those things
I cannot change.
I Accept.

Visualisation

With closed eyes and a tranquil mind
Imagine your Acceptance of all
you see and experience:
See yourself on awakening,
Accepting the way you feel,
Your anticipation of the day,
the weather and all you
encouter on your path.
On proceeding through the day,
see yourself
Accepting the challenges
and apparent obstacles that present.
Imagine yourself Accepting
the people you encounter
and the results of activities experienced.
The world events and the things you cannot change.
See yourself Accepting
all that comes your way with a
tranquil mind and acceptance will be yours.

Trust

Trust is the confidence in
and reliance on
good qualities,
especially fairness, truth,
honour or ability.
Trust is a big test
at any time
for any one.
Trust
can make
us feel vulnerable.
Trust
is necessary
for us to function
in Love.
If we listen
to our inner-voice
and stay
"in love" we can
Trust
and grow in safety.

Affirmation

Each day
in every day
I Trust.
I listen
to my innate
inner wisdom
and know
that the choices I make
are made through
Trust.
with an open heart.
I Trust.

Visualisation

With closed eyes and a tranquil mind
Imagine yourself in a state of Trust.
See yourself having the inner wisdom
to Trust your instincts
and intuition.
Imagine Trusting that all
is as it is meant to be.
See yourself Trusting
that you are being guided
each and every step of the way
on your path in life with
Trust.

Present

The present is taking place
or existing now.
At all times
be
Present.
From the moment
you awaken.
Determine
to be fully
Present.
Each and every task
throughout the day
should have
undivided attention.
Being aware
and fully focused.
We should view our world
and the world at large
holistically.
No matter where we are
or what we are doing.
Be focused
and
Present.

Affirmation

Each day
in every day
I am
Focused
and
Present.
I welcome
each new day
as a precious
Present.
I am
Present.

Visualisation

With closed eyes and a tranquil mind
Imagine yourself being
Present.
In your mind your are totally
Present at all times.
Imagine yourself not in the
past or the future.
See yourself present in the
"precious Present"
therefore enjoying
all it has to offer you.

Dignity

Dignity is a proper sense
of pride and self-respect.
One of the
principle morals
of some faiths
is allowing
Dignity.
For an elderly person
to lose Dignity
is paramount in their life.
For a child to lose
Dignity
is soul crushing
and leads to
low self-esteem.
Dignity
separates us
from lesser species.
Dignity
allows us to hold
our head high.
with Pride and Dignity.

Affirmation

Each day
in every day
I allow others
and myself
the right of
Dignity.
I hold my head high
and treat all
with respect, thus
allowing their
Dignity
to stay in tact
at all times.
I allow Dignity.
I am
Dignified.

Visualisation

With closed eyes and a tranquil mind
Imagine Dignity
as a base from which to function.
See yourself as
Dignified at all times,
acting with Dignity.
See the
Dignity in all living things.
Be rewarded by becoming more
Dignified with each day.

Being

Being is the state
of existing.
Love is just
Being.
Being who we are.
Being an
example to others.
Being
happy, healthy,
successful,
and prosperous.
Being loving.
Being
a human being
in love
just simply
Being.

Affirmation

Each day in every way,
I am who I am, not who people
may expect me to be.
I am
Being.
Loving, kind,
compassionate,
understanding,
knowledgeable,
wise, successful,
prosperous, talented,
courageous, confident,
ambitious, serene and calm
in the understanding
that I am happy
Being
me.
I am at one
with all things.
I am
Being.

Visualisation

With closed eyes and a tranquil mind
Imagine Being
what you would like to be.
See your inner Being or spirit
becoming more enlightened.
Imagine Being more powerful,
yet serene.
See yourself Being who you truly are,
and proud of it
Imagine Being all you can be,
all you were meant to be.
See yourself tap into your inner self and
Be who you really are.

Love Verse

As I gaze into my eyes.
I see my heart, I see my size.
I see the light within my soul.
The infinite reflection of the whole.

The soul of eternity in physical form.
Consciousness experiencing life re-born.
I ask for guidance on my chosen way.
Each step, as I grow from day to day.

In this world of many choices.
Many challenges many voices.
May I hear the voice that really matters
and not the idle mental chatters.

That of the infinite from "above".
Through intuition with love as I am loved
I see within your soul so near.
A reflection of myself so clear.

As we are units of the whole.
Not just a body and mind but a soul.
Reflecting the light of the infinite power.
Experiencing and learning hour by hour.

As we spend each moment of each day.
Let us reflect and ponder come what may.
On the love we consider in each smiling face.
Open hearts waiting to experience the grace.

Of the purity of the light of love.
The gentleness and softness of the pure white dove.
It's there for the asking, nothing to prove.
All we have to do is share our love.

Love is everywhere, we just need to look.
Reflected in nature, people, animals, a book.
A painitng, a photograph, a poem a word.
An expression, a sigh, hug, a kiss, assured.

Love is intangible, but the expression is clear.
Love is positive, trust, faith eliminating fear.
Compassion, generosity, understanding and grace.
The truth and empathy in a loving face.

The choice is there to use each day.
Love or hate black, white or gray.
Love comes easily when we remember to choose,
To give a hug and not abuse

Those whom we love with whom we share.
Our days and lives with thought and care.
Love costs nothing it's there, it's free.
Love is all that is - all we need to be.
Share your Love.

Lynn Merrin © 2024

teen SERENITY guide

by LYNN MERRIN

Introduction

Serenity is an inspiring book designed to
assist you to make positive change in your life.

Take a personal journey of consideration,
beyond the physical,
to further understand the subconscious
mind from a metaphysical viewpoint.

Confidence is the first of four motivational guides,
complete with inspiring verses,
daily affirmations and creative visualisations.
These verses are charged with Reiki energy to enhance
these personally empowering processes.

Serenity

This book is designed
to encourage the reader
to contemplate
the meaning
and aspects of
Serenity
in relation to the self
and life generally.
The Affirmation and
Visualisation for
Serenity
can be used daily
and affirmed audibly
to empower the words
and the meaning of
Serenity
in our life.
The verse has been added
for your enjoyment
The book and contents
have been charged
with the Universal energy of
Reiki.

Looking at the various aspects
of expression of serenity
we consider the following

Serenity	Is a state of mind and a state of being
Peace	comes with faith, trust and acceptance
Wisdom	comes with knowledge, experience and choices
Knowledge	comes with learning and experiencing
Love	comes unconditionally
Compassion	feeling for others with understanding
Understanding	knowing on an inner level what is
Acceptance	knowing that all is happening as it should
Faith	trusting in the universe and all that is
Trust	believing in ourselves and all that is
Music	inspires the soul
Colours	tranquil colours of serenity sooth
The Sea	immersing ourselves in natures calm
Bath	taking aromatic baths
Time	taking the time to do nothing
Breath	breathing deeply and mindfully

Contemplate
the meaning
and aspects
of "Serenity"
in relation to the self
and life generally.
The Affirmation and
Visualisation
for "Serenity"
should be used daily
and affirmed audibly
to empower the words
and the meaning
of "Serenity".
The verses have been added
for your enjoyment.

Serenity

Is being free of stress, worry or disturbance.
Having the
wisdom and experience to know
that we are complete as a unit of the
whole of creation.
That we also create each day of our lives
and we are master of our destiny.
Serenity can be achieved through
mind meditation,
aromatic baths,
and listening to classical music,
Focusing on soothing colours.
watching dolphins frolic in the sea.
Watching children sleeping.
Just sitting and contemplating
doing nothing at all.
Serenity is a state of mind and a learned art
Non-attachment, acceptance,
faith, trust, peace, all lead to
Serenity.
The colours green and blue can be a
Serene focus
and be soothing
to the wearer of clothing
made from these colours.
Breathing deeply
can also maintain
Serenity as a state of mind.

Affirmation

Each day
In every way,
I am more
Serene.
As I accept my experiences
and lessons in life
with grace,
wisdom,
faith and trust.
I know that in
the divine plan of life,
that all is happening
as it should.
No matter
whether good or bad,
each experience
will pass
with the ebb and flow
of time, as I grow more
Serene
I am Serene.

Visualisation

Visualise yourself being
Serene at all times.
See yourself emanating
Serenity for all to enjoy.
Visualise this
Serenity filling every cell
of your body and passing
from you to all
you encounter.
See yourself as
Serene.

Peace

Peace is a state of mental
calm and serenity.
Serenity is having
Peace
Our our heart no matter
what is happening in our life.
Knowing deep within us
that as there are
ebbs and flows in nature,
so to, will we experience
highs and lows in our life.
At all times,
We have the choice to choose
Peace.
When we choose peace, it emanates
from us and influences others
and our environment.
As a pebble in the pond
we find
Peace.

Affirmation

Each day in every way,
I find Peace.
With Peace
I am at one
with the laws of nature.
I acknowledge
the ebb and flows
in my life and
I embrace them in
Peace.
I create a
Peaceful
space
wherever I am so
my mind and emotions are
Peaceful.
I have Peace
I am at Peace.

Visualisation

With closed eyes and a tranquil mind
See yourself Peaceful at all times,
with all you encounter.
Imagine yourself wrapped
in a blanket of Peace,
where nothing can disturb your being.
Visualise yourself approaching everything
and everyone with
Peace
in your heart,
your mind and emotions
and you will be
Peaceful.

Wisdom

Wisdom is the knowledge and experience
needed to make
sensible decisions and judgements,
or the good sense
shown by sensible decisions and
judgements.
Serenity is acknowledging
the innate
Wisdom of the Universe.
Not necessarily the physically learned,
but the spiritually known
Wisdom
Within and without.
Wisdom is deeply contained
and known as an invaluable gift.
The Wise need not display
their Wisdom
In Serenity.

Affirmation

Each day
In every way
I know that
Wisdom
Is within me
as it is around me.
The Universal Energy
holds all information,
past present and
future for me to access,
as required.
I am
Wise.

Visualisation

With closed eyes and a tranquil mind,
Visualise yourself
pausing before
responding to any situation
and
considering the circumstances
with Wisdom.
See yourself drawing on the deep inner
Wisdom
that is innately
who you truly are.

Knowledge

Knowledge is general awareness,
or possession
of information, facts, ideas,
truths or principles.
Serenity is
Knowledge
acquired through experience,
learning and accessing
the wisdom within.
Knowledge allows us the
peace and serenity to
go about our daily lives without
having to prove ourselves.
Knowledge is Knowing.
Knowing how to live successfully,
happily and healthily
Knowing how to manage finances,
home, career, family
Knowing how to engage in various activities,
events and relaxation.
Knowing allows serenity.
Libraries are free,
the internet is inexpensive,
Inner Knowledge is innate.

Affirmation

Each day
in every way
I acknowledge
my
Knowledge.
Knowing that I learn
as I grow.
Every experience, and
lesson in life gives me
Knowledge.
I embrace Knowledge
I Know.

Visualisation

With closed eyes and a tranquil mind
Visualise yourself drawing on your
Knowledge
at each encounter.
See yourself with the ability to
recall information,
neatly filed in your
subconscious mind.
Visualise all that inner
Knowledge at the ready
whenever you require it.
See yourself as all Knowing
and remember
to educate, is to "draw out"
inner knowledge,

Love

Love is an intense feeling of tender
affection and compassion.
Serenity is having
Love
In our heart for ourselves,
our fellow man,
nature and all that is.
Knowing that we are a part
of all that is,
we can love all.
Knowing that
Love
Is the most harmonious
vibration to enhance
our well being
and hold us
In a state of
Serenity.
We can stay in a state of
Love
to stay
Serene.

Affirmation

Each day
in every way
I love.
I show Love,
I hold, Love
In my heart
and all that I do and say
Is acted out of
Love.
I love
and
Love brings
Serenity
I Love.

Visualisation

With closed eyes and a tranquil mind
Visualise yourself
acting from a place of
Love at all times.
No matter the circumstance,
be the "bigger person"
and see yourself being a
Loving individual,
choosing
Love over fear
at all times.

Compassion

Compassion is sympathy for the
suffering of others,
often with a desire to help.
Serenity is having
Compassion
for others on our path.
We are all on
different paths and
differing stages of each path.
We are all where we
are meant to be,
but at times we each can
suffer in our passage through
the challenges of life.
We can have
Compassion for those
who are experiencing hardship
and offer them understanding
and help if they ask.
Compassion is heart felt and
must come from the heart.

Affirmation

Each day
In every way,
I feel
Compassion
for my
fellow man and
all living things.
As they experience
any hardship,
I offer support
to all who come
to me in need.
I am
Compassionate.

Visualisation

With closed eyes and a tranquil mind
Visualise yourself acting with
Compassion
every day in any
situation where another is
suffering on any level.
See yourself understanding
with empathy and
Compassion.

Understanding

Understanding is the ability to perceive
and explain the meaning
or the nature of somebody or something.
Serenity is having
Understanding
Of what is.
Knowing deep within us
that each person has
designed his or her life plan
on a subconscious level.
We are experiencing that
plan in accord with
those chosen to
share the experience.
When anyone comes to us
seeking our assistance
we show
Understanding of their
needs and empathise with their situation
and circumstance without judgement,
showing
Understanding.

Affirmation

Each day
In every way
I Understand
the way of the Universe
and my role within that plan.
I show
Understanding in
each and every thing I do.
I listen to instruction,
and make sure I
Understand.
I listen to the stories of others
and I show
Understanding.

Visualisation

With closed eyes and a tranquil mind
Visualise yourself
Understanding the other
person's point of view or the
situation at hand.
See yourself
truly listening and
seeing the other persons'
point of view with
Understanding.

Acceptance

Acceptance is the willingness to believe
that something is true.
Serenity is being
Accepting
of what is.
Remaining detached.
Knowing that we have
chosen our path and
our lessons on this journey,
as have others on their path.
We understand that things are
happening as they should,
regardless of how they may
appear to be
in terms of our reality.
Acceptance
brings us
Serenity.

Affirmation

Each day
In every way,
I Accept
that all is
as it is meant to be.
At any time in
any place,
I remain
detached with
compassion and
Understanding.
I Accept.

Visualisation

With closed eyes and a tranquil mind
Visualise yourself
Understanding the
point of view of the other person,
or the situation at hand.
See yourself truly
listening and
seeing their
point of view
with an open heart and with
Understanding.

Trust

Trust is confidence in and reliance on
good qualities, especially, fairness,
truth, honour or ability.
Serenity is
Trusting
that each
person will come to
realise that they are fulfilling
their mission in life.
Accepting with love and
embracing the challenges
and Joys experienced
With Trust.
Trust
knows no fear.

Affirmation

Each day in every way
I Trust.
I Trust
that I am in the right
place at the right time,
with the right people,
doing the right thing for me.
I Trust
I am loving, caring,
accepting, compassionate
calm, understanding,
Trusting and faithful, always.
I am serene
and
I Trust.

Visualisation

With closed eyes and a tranquil mind
Visualise yourself
Trusting
with your inner being.
See yourself
Trusting things to unfold,
as they should,
guided by your inner Serene
wisdom with
Trust.

Music

Music is sounds usually produced
by voice or instruments,
that are
arranged or played in order
to create
a pleasing or stimulating effect.
Classical, Baroque, and Ambient
music are conducive
to relaxation and
Serenity.
Music has been used
throughout the ages
as a source of relaxation, to
promote a state of
Serenity.

Affirmation

Each day in every way
I hear Music.
I know that
Music
soothes my soul and
Uplifts my spirit,
Therefore I listen to
Music daily for fun,
relaxation or inspiration.
I appreciate
Music.
Music feeds
my soul.

Visualisation

With closed eyes and a tranquil mind
Visualise Music being
a part of your life.
See your spirit lifted
by the vibration of
classical Music,
nurtured by love songs,
energised by popular
Music.
See Music fill each and
every cell of your body
as a quality vibration
for healing and
regeneration.

Colour

Colour is the property of objects that depends
on the light that they reflect and that is perceived as
red, blue, yellow and shades and hues thereof.
Colour guides our moods as we choose
fabrics to dress our bodies and our
residences and work places.
The blues and greens are Serene.
Colour is all around us
and plays a large role in the
psychology of
our lives.
The colours of nature are
Serene.

Affirmation

Each day in every way
I use Colour
I wear Colour to express my persona
and to reflect my mood.
I use Colour in my home
to enhance the atmosphere
and character of each room.
My garden or balcony is filled
with the Colour of nature.
I love having
Colour in my life,
as an expression of who I am.

Visualisation

With closed eyes and a tranquil mind
Visualise Colour as your expression
of serenity.
See yourself in Colours of greens,
blues, pastels and any
Colour that makes
you feel and appear to be
Serene.

The Sea

That great body of water that
surrounds our lands and covers
approximately 70 per cent
of the earth.
Exhilarating to swim in and
has excellent health properties
The Sea, rivers, lakes and streams
are soothing
to watch and
a great source of Serenity
for those privileged
to live beside or visit them.
These waterways are a great
relaxer and a wonderful
source of meditative
contemplation.

Affirmation

Each day in every way
I acknowledge The Sea, rivers,
lakes and streams.
Whether a walk on the beach
by a lake, river or stream.
Viewing a painting,
Meditating or reminiscing
I remember
and refer to
these waterways and their
majestic beauty.

Visualisation

With closed eyes and a tranquil mind
Visualise yourself swimming in the Sea,
a lake, river or steam.
See nature supporting
you and lifting you
over the waves as
the salt water cleanses
your body and aura and
the experience cleanses
your mind and emotions.
See yourself having fun
in these waters of
of Serenity.

The Bath

The bath is the act of immersing
all or part of the body in a
bathtub in order to wash it.
Bathing has not only been a form of
hygiene through the ages, but also an
act of somewhat decadence.
Cleopatra bathed in milk with
maidens to wash her body
and attend to her every need.
Today we have an abundance of hot
water and scented oils at our disposal.
Add some candles and music and
the scene is set for
Serenity.

Affirmation

Each day in every way
I bathe.
I know that Bathing
is a wonderful form
of relaxation and cleansing.
Whether in a bath
or shower ,
river or stream,
I enjoy bathing
to wash my body,
my mind and
my spirit.

Visualisation

With closed eyes and a tranquil mind
Visualise yourself soaking in a hot,
aromatic Bath,
sprinkled with rose petals,
as you listen to your favourite music
and read your favourite book.
Or
just relax by candlelight.
See yourself as essentially
Serene following
this relaxing Bath.

Time

Time is a dimension
that enables two identical
events occurring
at the same point
in space
to be distinguished, or measured
by the interval between events.
Whilst we measure time in our world,
it is believed
by some ancient cultures,
that all time is
occurring simultaneously.
However we use time,
we should acknowledge it,
for what it is,
a measure.

Affirmation

Each day in every way
I acknowledge Time.
I know that time is precious.
I stay in the moment,
honouring time and
I respect other's time.
I am aware of
Time and the role
it plays in
my life.

Visualisation

With closed eyes and
a tranquil mind
Visualise yourself
always having Time.
See yourself being on
Time for all occasions.
See Time as a measure
of your progress
and success.
See your self at
one with
time.

Breath

Breath is the air
that a person
or animal inhales
and exhales.
Conscious breath, enables
not only oxygenation
of our systems, but
relaxation of our body,
our mind and
our spirit.
Deep breathing
enables calm,
by relaxing
the body and mind,
especially
in times of stress.

Affirmation

Each day in every way,
I am aware of my Breath.
I remember to Breathe
when a stressful
situation arises.
My breathing is rhythmic,
at all times.
I Breath fresh air
to fuel my
body and clear
my mind.
I am aware of my
Breath at all times.
I breathe deeply.

Visualisation

With closed eyes and
a tranquil mind,
Visualise yourself Breathing
into your lower,
then your upper diaphragm
and then your lungs.
See yourself Breathing
clean air into your body
and exhaling stale air,
as you Breathe.
See yourself conscious
of every Breath
as you fill your body
with oxygenating life,
to renew your cells.

Serenity Verse

As I contemplate a sunrise at dawn
I wonder at the creator born
Of love in a universe in toil.
To create our planet, to not be spoiled.

Wondering at the power of nature, the tragedy of man
The Universe represented in a grain of sand.
I pray that each soul may find it in their heart
To care for our planet, each individual doing their part

To restore the balance we have lost
Before we suffer the ultimate cost
Of the final destruction of the consciousness of man
Find the balance in Serenity and understand.

Serenity is found in the rising sun.
The mother feeding, the job well done.
The swan on the lake the bird on the wing.
The monk in meditation the child on the swing.

Serenity, just a state of mind.
A choice in life, a way to find.
The easy way to navigate the course
Through life when things may get worse.

The reflection on the inner mind.
The strength to go within, wisdom to find.
The truth in Serenity, the healing, the state
Of peace, tranquillity, the sanctum, the grace.

Serenity is there to enjoy.
Born within each girl and boy.
Lost throughout the riggers of time.
Time to find again the fine line.

Between turmoil and peace, the choice is ours
To take time out, to smell the flowers.
Time to enjoy the beauty around
Be still, let it pass by, let Serenity surround.

Life is much easier when Serenity is used.
Reflected in the faced of those who choose
To integrate Serenity into their days
To integrate Serenity into their ways.

Of looking at life and all that it holds.
Of ways to meet challenges and so we are told.
That Serenity is a way to be
To just live life in Serenity.

© Lynn Merrin 2024.

Peace Verse

As we search for peace, we are bound to find.
Peace is elusive, peace not the kind
Of thing we find, when looking outside,
But within, more the point, along for the ride.

No point in searching out side of ourselves
For the peace, in peaceful places, instead to delve
Within, we ultimately we have to live
Where ultimately peace, has all to give.

Time taken to spend, in quiet contemplation.
Time to consider, the state of the nation.
The state of the world, and all considered
Time to reflect on messages delivered.

Peace can be found, in a peaceful place.
Peace, we find in a peaceful face.
Peace, a learned experience, not to be found,
Searching the sky, searching the found

Peace, is a state of mind, no matter what
Is happening around us, what is, what is not.
Peace, regardless of happy or sad
Peace is within, Peace to be glad.

Find your piece of peace today.
Find your peace, when others say
Hurtful things, to make you react
Angry words, when it's they in fact

Who need to find peace, not matter the scene
No matter the conflict, pull back the screen
and face what it is, with peace in your heart
Difficult at first, but a fine place to start.

Peace is a discipline, a choice to be made.
Peace versus conflict, the worries to fade.
As peace then becomes, a way of living
Peace then is the state, peace the giving.

© Lynn Merrin 2024.

Desiderada

"Go placidly amid the noise and the haste, and remember what peace there may be in silence. As far as possible, without surrender, be on good terms with all persons. Speak your truth quietly and clearly; and listen to others, even the dull and ignorant; They too have their story. Avoid loud and aggressive persons; they are vexatious to the spirit. If you compare yourself with others, you may become vain or bitter, for always there will be greater and lesser persons than yourself. Enjoy your achievements as well as your plans. Keep interested in your own career, however humble; It is a real possession in the changing fortunes of time. Exercise caution in your business affairs, for the world is full of trickery. But let this not blind you to what virtue there is; Many persons strive for high ideals, and everywhere life is full of heroism. Be yourself. Especially do not feign affection. Neither be cynical about love; for in the face of all aridity and disenchantment it is as perennial as the grass. Take kindly the council of the years, Gracefully surrendering the things of youth. Nurture strength of spirit to shield you in sudden misfortune. But do not distress yourself with dark imagining. Many fears are born of fatigue and loneliness. Beyond a healthy discipline, Be gentle with yourself. You are a child of the universe no less than the trees and the stars; you have a right to be here, no doubt the universe is unfolding as it should. Therefore, be at peace with God, Whatever you conceive Him to be, and whatever your labours and aspirations, in the noisy confusion of life, keep peace in your soul. With all its sham, drudgery, and broken dreams, it is still a beautiful world. Be cheerful.
Strive to be happy."

Author Unknown although some maintain that this piece was written by Max Erhmann.

The Seven Principles of Hawaiian Huna

Your world is a reflection of what you believe.

1. Ike.

The world is what you think it is.
Your world is a reflection of what you believe.

2. Kala.

"There are no limits".
Everything is connected, anything is possible

3. Makia.

"Energy flows where attention goes".
You get what you focus on

4. Manawa.

"Now is the moment of power".
Everything is relative.
Power increases with senory attention.

5. Aloha.

"To love is to be happy with".
Love increases as judgement decreases.
Everything is alive, aware and responsive.
Criticism in any form weakens you.

6. Mana.

"All power comes from within".
Everything has power. Power comes from authority.
All power comes from within you

7. Pono.

"Effectiveness is the measure of truth".
There is always another way to do anything

"Yesterday is history, tomorrow a mystery; today a gift. That's why it is the present"
May your attitudes be flexible, loving and with the greatest good of all in mind.

Confidence
Ambition
Love and
Serenity

Are four individual books and
Take the reader on a journey of
consideration beyond the physical.
Expanding the conscious mind
and impressing the subconscious
with daily Affirmation and Visualisation.

Each book is complete with poem and charged
with Reiki energy.

Lynn Merrin
Psychotherapy Counselor
Bachelor of Metaphyisics and Reiki Master
Has studied
Natural and Vibrational Therapies and
Neurolinguistic Programing/Hypnotherapy
since 1986

For further information
www.lynnmerrin.com.au

This book is dedicated to my children
Kylie and Damien
© Lynn Merrin 2024.

a compilation
OF HOW TO
HAVE MORE

confidence

ambition

love

serentiy

by **LYNN MERRIN**

roduct-compliance

20